Eric Otis Simmons

Information provided in #HTSP - How to Self-Publish is intended to serve as a resource or "primer" for getting started in self-publishing. However, there is no guaranty that self-publishing of any book or other written or spoken language publication will generate any income or guaranty results. In addition to the lack of any guaranty, express or implied, there is also no express or implied Warranty. Purchaser or any third party that receives this publication from a purchaser hereby acknowledges and agrees that the Author makes no representation or warranty, express or implied, at law or in equity, in any respect to any matter relating to the contents of this publication including, without limitation, any strategy, course of action, or other undertaking.

The Purchaser hereby waives any and all claims that may arise as a result of any actions or other activities or lack of same by the Purchaser on any third party that may or may not have resulted from the content contained within this Publication. Purchaser agrees to indemnify and defend the Author, the Author's representatives, heirs, assigns or designees against any and all claims by the Purchaser of any third party.

#HTSP - How to Self-Publish

Copyright © 2018 by Eric Simmons Enterprises, Inc.

All rights are reserved. No part of this book may be reproduced or transmitted in any form or by any means without written permission from the author.

ISBN 9780578409467

# Dedication

This book is dedicated to my wife Cynthia as we celebrate our 39$^{th}$ wedding anniversary this year. Without question, you're the best thing that has ever happened to me. You keep me grounded, and for that, I thank you. You are my best friend, and I sincerely appreciate you for all of your love and support over the years.

# Acknowledgments

Many thanks to Carla Burton, Branch Manager of the Dr. Robert E. Fulton Library in Johns Creek, Georgia for suggesting I develop a presentation to share information with others about how I was able to successfully self-publish my first book. Carla's recommendation spawned the creation of "#HTSP – How to Self-Publish."

Thanks also to Michael McCree for reviewing this book. As a "Best Selling" Author, Michael's self-publishing acumen, insight, and ideas continue to inspire and keep me motivated about self-publishing.

## About the Author

Eric Otis Simmons was born in Little Rock, Arkansas and moved to Montgomery, Alabama at the age of 13 with his Mother who raised him as a single parent. He went on to graduate from **Auburn University** where he finished in the **Top 10% of his class** (B.S. Business Administration, Marketing minor) and earned Varsity Basketball letters as a 5' 7" walk-on player.

After College, Simmons spent a little over three decades in Corporate America in various Sales/Sales Management roles with Fortune 500 employers **IBM, AT&T, GE, MCI** and **W.W. Grainger**. At IBM, he was named "Class President" of the Company's then world-renowned Sales Training Program and appeared on a WSFA-TV live broadcast entitled, "Blacks in Corporate America." His domestic and international business travels took him to 37 states and also Paris, Brussels and Hong Kong where he successfully closed sales of **$500,000, $1 million**, and **$25 million** respectively. During his AT&T tenure, Simmons was featured in Black Enterprise Magazine's "Powerplay" section in an article entitled, "The new deal on business entertaining."

About the Author

A **Certified Wix Webmaster**, Simmons started his own website development company, Eric Simmons Enterprises, Inc. (ESE, Inc.) in 2017. The company builds "Personal Brand" websites for High School Student-Athletes to help them get recruited by College Coaches. ESE, Inc. utilizes Simmons' Copyrighted **EC3 Continuum** methodology to assist Student-Athletes and their Parents with the critical stages of Engaging Coaches (for Recruiting), Engaging Colleges (for Admission), and Engaging Companies (for Employment).

After roughly 15 years of people urging him to write a book about his life, in March 2017, Simmons released his popular self-published Memoir, "**Not Far From The Tree**." The book is dedicated to his Mother and speaks to the invaluable "seeds of knowledge" she instilled in him that enabled him to accomplish some incredible things in life, despite seemingly impossible odds.

At the time of publication of, "#HTSP – How to Self-Publish," 25 Libraries had acquired Simmons' Memoir, 7 of which are amongst the largest in the Nation. The most notable being the New York Public Library which ordered his Memoir for its prestigious Schomburg Center for Research in Black Culture.

About the Author

Not Far From The Tree and #HTSP – How to Self-Publish
Website - www.esetomes.com
Facebook - www.faceBook.com/esimmonsauthor

ESE, Inc.
Website – www.eseinc1.com
Facebook - www.faceBook.com/ESE-Inc-1431136640304095/?ref=br_rs

# Contents

| | | |
|---|---|---|
| Dedication | | iii |
| Acknowledgments | | iv |
| About the Author | | v |
| Contents | | viii |
| Why #HTSP? | | ix |
| Chapter 1 | My First Self-Published Book | 1 |
| Chapter 2 | Publisher versus Self-Publishing | 4 |
| Chapter 3 | Getting Started Writing | 8 |
| Chapter 4 | Writing Your Book | 26 |
| Chapter 5 | Setting up Your Book Business | 40 |
| Chapter 6 | Identifying Initial Service Providers | 42 |
| Chapter 7 | Pricing Your Book | 52 |
| Chapter 8 | Formatting Your Book for Printing | 55 |
| Chapter 9 | Marketing Your Book | 67 |
| Chapter 10 | Managing Your Book Business | 75 |
| Chapter 11 | Can You Make Money Self-Publishing? | 79 |
| References | | 81 |

# Why #HTSP?

1. A little over a year after its release, Eric Simmons' self-published Memoir, "Not Far From The Tree," his first book, had been ranked in the **"Top 1%" 25 times** and in the **"Top 10%" 104 times** out of over 8,000,000 books sold worldwide on Amazon.com. From 2017 to 2018, **sales of Simmons' Memoir grew 69% year over year.**

2. Without paying for expensive book reviews, Simmons was able to convince 25 Libraries, some of which are amongst America's foremost Academic and Public Libraries, to procure his self-published Memoir not long after contacting them about the book.

3. #HTSP takes the reader through the methodology Simmons used when he self-published his popular first book.

## Why #HTSP?

4. #HTSP can be used as a "reference tool" or **"primer"** for:
   - First-time Self-Publishers
   - People interested in learning more about Self-Publishing

# Chapter 1
# My First Self-Published Book

Perhaps you are in the same "place" as I was several years ago. You've decided to write a book, and you think you want to self-publish it, yet you don't have a clue about where or how to begin. Looking back, over a 12-year period, I procrastinated at least 12 times before I built up the courage to write my first book. I had a story burning inside of me that I wanted to get out, but I kept coming up with all types of excuses to keep from getting started. Finally, in 2016, I sat down and crafted my first book. I did so without any prior knowledge whatsoever about book writing or the book publishing industry. Part of my motivation to finally start my writing stemmed from me having just turned 60 years old. Not knowing how much time I had left on this earth, I figured I better get busy writing my book before my time ran out. It was a matter of checking off my "bucket list," so to speak before I kicked the bucket!

A storyteller by nature, people would often tell me they found my life stories funny and fascinating. From sisters-in-law (Mary and Juanita) to co-workers to friends, I was encouraged to write a book about my life, and subsequently, I did. At the outset, I had several goals for my Memoir. First, not having a lot of information about my family history, I was determined to leave material behind for my children and their children's children about our heritage. Second, I wanted to give young people, who like me, may have been raised by a single Black parent, hope that they could achieve and overcome obstacles in life as I had done.

If current sales results and noteworthy clientele are indicators, it's safe to say; my first self-published book has been a success! What I have found most interesting throughout this process has been people's fascination with my having self-published a book. They automatically assume I went through a Publisher. I also get the feeling; some think I am "special" now because I'm in a book or because I have written one. I guess this "exalted one" perception, real or imagined, comes from the "prestige" associated with books.

After it became apparent to me that there is indeed a need out there for "**current**" and "**concise**" information on self-publishing, especially from someone who's recently done it, I decided to write "#HTSP – How to Self-Publish" to help you and others get started in self-publishing. In this book, I will share with you steps I undertook to successfully self-

## Chapter 1 — My First Self-Published Book

publish my first book and this one. My goal is to provide you with an informative tool that is less than 100 pages. The average for this type of book is 181 pages! My objective is to shorten your self-publishing learning curve so that you can spend more of your time writing your book and less time educating yourself like I did when I was working on my first book. With that as a backdrop, let's begin!

# Chapter 2
## Publisher versus Self-Publishing

Before I began writing my first book, I was pretty sure I wanted to self-publish the piece. To be on the safe side, however, I did a lot of Google research to gain an understanding of the differences between going through a publisher versus self-publishing. Through research, I felt I would either validate or invalidate my self-publishing decision. Almost immediately, I found out there is a plethora of information on publishing versus self-publishing on the Internet. So much so, I was overwhelmed. Fortunately, I came across an article, "Pros And Cons Of Traditional Publishing vs. Self-Publishing," written by best-selling Author Joanna Penn who had transitioned from the traditional Publisher route to Self-Publishing. Based on Penn's information, I created a T-Chart with Publisher on the left side and Self-Publish on the right. Underneath each mode of publishing, I listed the pros and cons. Being a "visual learner," seeing information in this format would help me get to a final decision regarding how I was going to publish my book.

During my research, I also came across an exercise that I tried. It was to think of your favorite book. Then, contemplate on who the Author was of the book and lastly, think about who published the book. For the life of me, I couldn't name the specific Publisher of any book I'd read! It was at that point; perhaps, when I began to question the significance of a Publisher. When I concluded my research, I was able to validate "Self-Publishing" as the best route for me to take regarding my book. For me, the "Pros" far outweighed the "Cons."

## Decision # 1 - Publisher or Self-Publish

### Publisher

**Pros**
- Prestige
- Sales to Bookstores

**Cons**
- Slow Process (1-2 Years to Launch)
- Royalties 7%-25% (generously)
- Agents/Contracts
- May be Complex

### Self-Publish

**Pros**
- Control and Faster Time to Market
- Higher Royalties
  - Mine: 16%-70% (Kindle)
- Rights Retention
- Pick who you sell to/through

**Cons**
- Everything is On You
- Stigma Due to Poor Works
- May Need Editor/Designer

Following are notes from my research:

# Publisher

**Pros**

- Prestige
- Distribution to bookstores via Sales Representatives
- An Advance (i.e., upfront money) to the Author
  Note: Per Penn, "...the advance is against royalties, which are usually 7-25% of net book price. Royalties can be 10% on average. So, if you get an advance of $10,000, you then have to earn more than $10,000 out of your royalty rate on your book sales before you get any more money."

**Cons**

- Slow process. Could take 1-2.5 years before book launch
- Royalties 7-25% with the latter being generous. Hard to predict cash flow
- Involves Contracts and could be complex
- May need an Agent

# Self-Publishing

**Pros**

- Total "**creative <u>control</u>**" over content and design
- Faster time to Market!
- Higher Royalties. Note: Amazon Kindle can be up to 70%! Note: My current book royalties from all of my service providers range from 16-70%.
- Retain your rights
- Pick and choose who to sell your book to and through

**Cons**

- Virtually, everything is on you
- You may need to find:
    - A proofreader/editor
    - Cover Designer
- The "Stigma" around Self-Publishers (i.e., are you legit)
    - A lot of poorly written self-published books
- May be challenging to get into bookstores
- Might be hard to get noticed for literary awards

# Chapter 3
# Getting Started Writing

For me, the hardest part about writing my first book was getting started. From 2005 through 2017, per my records, I started and stopped writing my manuscript a total of 12 times, as mentioned. I also re-titled the book a total of 7 times. On September 25, 2016, I finally decided on a title. Why was I having such a hard time getting started?

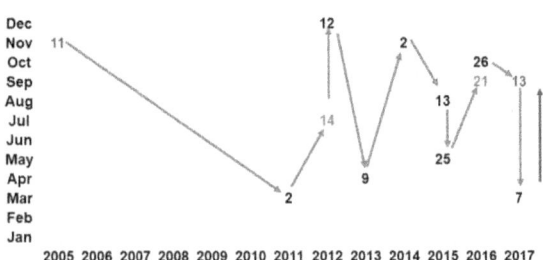

Why was I procrastinating? I was a seasoned sales professional with over thirty years of experience in Corporate America.

Chapter 3 　　　　　　　　　　Getting Started Writing

Writing emails, memos, etc. was something I did daily. I made so many excuses over the years for why I hadn't started writing my book, looking back now they are almost laughable. Two of my most common reasons were, "I'm too busy right now," and "I'll get around to it later." Chances are you've also been procrastinating about writing your book and probably for various reasons like mine. You are not alone, however. **According to a survey conducted by *The New York Times*, "81% of Americans feel they have a book in them - - and that they should write it."**

There are a lot of reasons why people perhaps procrastinate about writing their first book. Amongst those could be: fear of rejection, concern as to whether people will like the book, lack of confidence in one's writing skills, and others as indicated in the following chart:

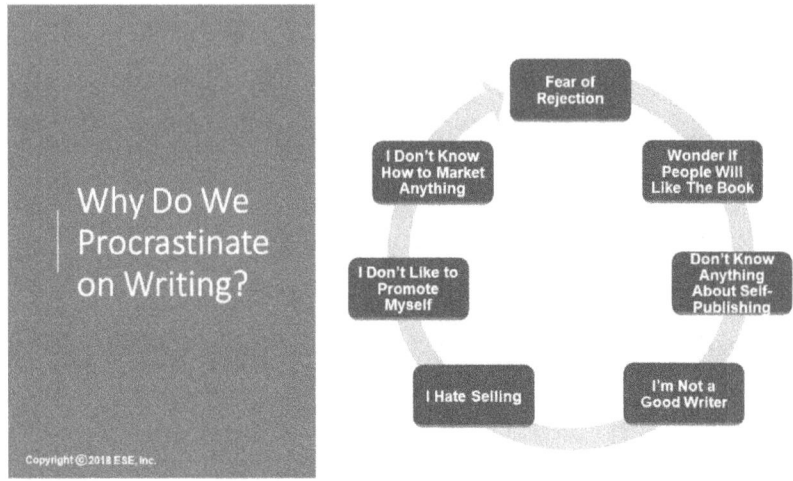

It wasn't until I took a hard look at why I wanted to write a book in the first place, that I was able to break the grip procrastination had on me.

## Identify Your Purpose for Writing

The way I overcame my book writing procrastination was by documenting why I was writing in the first place. I refer to this as my "Leap of Faith" moment. In my case, I was writing for my children. I had always yearned for detailed information about my lineage, but unfortunately, my Family's data was either extremely fragmented or non-existent. Relatives with knowledge of our Family's history had either

Chapter 3                    Identify Your Purpose for Writing

passed away, or forgotten information and very little was documented about our history. I was determined to learn as much about my family's genealogy and background as possible and provide my children with a "leave behind," so to speak. I also wanted to open up, a little bit, about myself to my children so they could understand what makes me tick. I made a conscious decision I would "bear my soul" to them, somewhat, with the caveat being, I sure as heck wasn't going to tell them everything! Some things are best left unsaid, and there may be something to the adage, "What goes on in Vegas, stays in Vegas" if you get my drift. I also believed my story of being raised by a single Black mother who inspired me to "success," would inspire and motivate young Black people, who like me, may have been raised by a single parent. Lastly, I felt if I did a quality job with my manuscript, I stood a chance of making a little bit of money from the book.

With my "true" purpose for writing laid out before me, I had the motivation and courage to proceed with writing my book. Going forward, whenever I found myself procrastinating, during my writing, I would refer back to my purpose!

Chapter 3                  Establish a Budget For Your Book

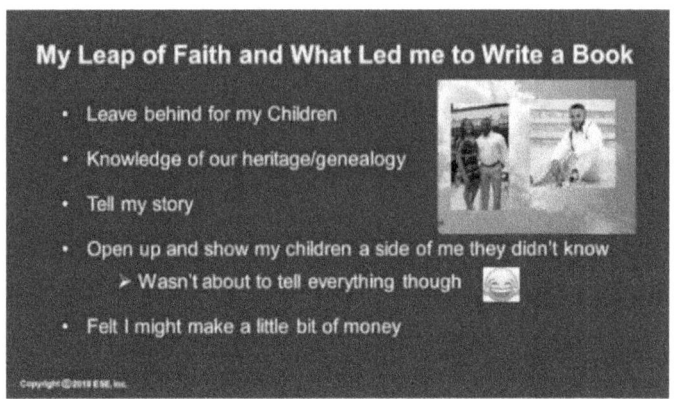

## Establish a Budget For Your Book

Taking a tip from Penn, one of the first things I did when I was getting started was to set a budget for how much I was going to invest in my book. I would encourage you to do the same because you will come to find, your costs can quickly add up.

I settled on a $500 budget for my first book because that was the maximum amount of money I was willing to take out of my personal funds for my project. This "financial structure" helped me avoid "unnecessary" expenses. Looking back at my accounting records, a year later, I was about $78 over budget for my first book.

For, "#HTSP – How to Self-Publish," I have set a budget of $300.00. Why am I budgeting lower than I did for

Chapter 3   Establish a Budget For Your Book

my first book? With roughly a year and a half of self-publishing experience under my belt, I have a better feel for what I can and can't live without cost wise. A critical area that I will be cutting back on is book "giveaways."

My #HTSP - How to Self-Publish Budget

| Description | Quantity | Estimated Cost |
|---|---|---|
| Universal ISBN | 1 | $99.00 |
| Ingram | 1 | $49.00 |
| Graphic Design | 1 | $50.00 |
| Advertising | 2 | $40.00 |
| Proof and Shipping (KDP, Ingram, Barnes & Noble) | 3 | $30.00 |
| Initial Inventory | 2 | $12.00 |
| Other | 1 | $20.00 |
| Total | | $300.00 |

The line items will become more apparent as you read through the book.

## Self-Publishing Jargon

As you begin to "walk the walk" in this new world of books, you'll need to be able to "talk the talk." Familiarizing yourself with some of the "Lingo" used in the book world will be beneficial to you. It will help boost your confidence as you begin to establish rapport with others and help you build credibility in the marketplace.

Without question, the most embarrassing thing that nearly happened to me, early on in my self-publishing journey, occurred after I had sent a Librarian some information about my first book. I received an email back saying the book had been sent over to the Library's Collection Department for review. I had an absolute panic attack! What in the world was going on, and why was the Library's Collection Department getting involved? I hadn't checked out a book from any Library nor did I owe one any money. I wasn't making a purchase that would require a credit review! Dumbfounded, I ran to Google for an answer. It turns out the term Collection(s) is used in the Library world to refer to the facility's books and other material. Imagine how embarrassing it would have been if I had called the Librarian and offered to provide her with my credit score!! In this section, I'll take you through a few key terms that nearly tripped me up to help you avoid a potentially embarrassing moment. In the book industry, you and I are often called **Independent Authors** or **Indies** or **Self-Publishers**. Because we are impacting their revenue stream, I would imagine some traditional publishing houses may refer to us in less flattering terms.

## Title

It may seem trivial, but I can't recall one person in the book industry ever asking me for the name of my book. They ask me for the book's title. Per Wikipedia, the title of a book, or any other published text or work of art, is a name for the work which is usually chosen by the Author.

## Genre

Admittedly, at the onset, I had no idea the significance of genre(s) in the book world. Ultimately, you're going to need to familiarize yourself with your book's category, and where it fits in the literary landscape. Why? A few reasons are: Your customers, such as a Library, for instance, may ask you the genre of your book. Also, from a sales perspective, your book's sales rankings in its genre will give you an idea of how your manuscript is doing as compared to other books in the same category. Familiarity with your book's genre will also help you with your marketing strategy, which I'll cover later.

Merriam-Webster defines genre as "a category of artistic, musical, or literary composition characterized by a particular style, form, or content." Per Wikipedia, genres fall into two categories, Fiction and Non-Fiction. According to Query*Tracker*, whose website states they help Authors find Literary Agents, based on all the genre information their users have supplied, Young Adult is the most popular Fiction genre while Memoirs top their list as the most popular Non-Fiction genre.

## Genres

| 10 Most Popular Fiction | 10 Most Popular Non-Fiction |
|---|---|
| 1 Young Adult | 1 Memoirs |
| 2 Fantasy | 2 Self-Help |
| 3 Children's | 3 Narrative |
| 4 Literary Fiction | 4 Religion/Spirituality |
| 5 Science Fiction | 5 Biography |
| 6 Thrillers/Suspense | 6 Cultural/Social Issues |
| 7 Middle Grade | 7 Business/Finance |
| 8 Romance | 8 History |
| 9 Picture Books | 9 General Non-Fiction |
| 10 Historical | 10 Health/Fitness |

Source: Query Tracker

As to revenue by genre, The Richest.com website states in a January 31, 2014 article by Thomas Stewart, "**Which 5 Book Genres Make The Most Money?**," the "Top 5" earning genres were:

1. Romance/Erotica - $1.44 billion
2. Crime/Mystery - $728.2 million
3. Religious/Inspirational - $720 million
4. Science Fiction/Fantasy - $590.2 million
5. Horror - $79.6 million

To see how the above $3.6 billion breaks out by percentages, I created the following pie chart.

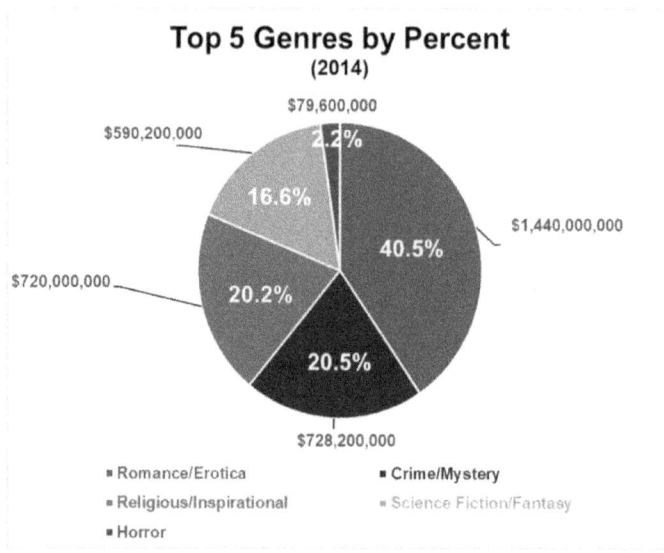

You can use this type of information to get a feel for the market potential of your book's genre.

## International Standard Book Number (ISBN)

The International Standard Book Number or ISBN is a unique numeric commercial book identifier. An ISBN is assigned to each edition and variation (except reprintings) of a book. Deciding on whether you're going to use an ISBN provided by the company(s) that will be printing and distributing your book or using a "Universal ISBN" will be an important decision for you. Currently, I have two ISBNs for the paperback version of my first book. My preference is to have only one ISBN but to get into specific markets I've chosen; I'm "stuck" with two ISBNs. I'll explain in Chapter 5 how I got into this conundrum. While having multiple sources for your customers to purchase your book through is great, having the same product with different ISBNs for ordering can confuse both your customers and yourself.

## Several Sites with Book Terminology

Should you come across a term or terms you don't understand; the following sites are helpful:

- authorHouse, "Book Publishing Terms" - https://www.authorhouse.com/AuthorResources/BookPublishingTerms.aspx

- Nathan Bransford, "Book publishing glossary" - https://blog.nathanbransford.com/book-publishing-glossary

- Bookjobs.com "Commonly Used Terms" - http://www.bookjobs.com/commonly-used-terms

## Self-Publishing Resources

If you were to do a Google search on how to self-publish, you would receive roughly 300 million hits. To save you time, I've put together a list of some of the most helpful resources I found when I was sitting in your shoes.

- Self Publishing Advice from the Alliance of Independent Authors -
  https://selfpublishingadvice.org/
  - This website is made available by the Alliance of Independent Authors or ALLi for short and is one of my favorite resources. ALLi is a non-profit professional association for authors who self-publish. You can search on the site for information on ISBNs for example and also find articles such as, "Book Production: 12 Avoidable Rookie Errors" by Debbie Young.

- The Creative Penn website -
  https://www.thecreativepenn.com/
  - Joanna Penn's website is filled with helpful information, a lot of which is free.

- The Indie View - http://www.theindieview.com/ - This website has a section called, "The Indie Reviewers List" which is where you can find a list of Independent Authors who have indicated their willingness to review fellow Indie Authors' book(s) for "Free." The Authors also state the genres they review. Before you start doing cartwheels, let me share with you my experience. For my first book, I contacted 16 reviewers, and I heard back from three. With such a low response rate, I had to remind myself, these individuals are Authors too, and they were probably busy writing their books. Before reaching out to each Author, one of the things I did was visit their websites. Not only did I want to learn more about the individual(s), I also wanted to get some ideas for my book's future site, which I planned on creating. Of the three Authors that I heard back from, Andreas Michaelides, a self-publisher based in Athens, Greece was the most accommodating. Andreas had written over twenty books at the time I reached out to him, and when he emailed me to make me aware he would review my book, he confirmed it would be for free. All he asked for in return was for me to review a book he had just finished. Although I had no previous book reviewing experience, I took advantage of the opportunity to learn about that side of the book business.

Fortunately, Andreas thoroughly enjoyed my book, as did I his, and he posted his review on Goodreads where he gave, "Not Far From The Tree," 5 stars. He also published his assessment and my bio on his website, Thirsty4Health for his European followers. The moral of the story is, keep digging to find a fellow Indie Author who is available to review your book for free. You may find a self-publishing Mentor and future friend along the way like I did with Andreas.

## Other Thoughts/Suggestions

- To restate, do review Authors' websites, particularly the successful ones. This includes those who use a traditional publisher and those who self-publish. As mentioned, this will give you ideas for your website and **show you how others are marketing their books**.

Chapter 3						Self-Publishing Resources

- Review Author Biographies on Amazon.com. Reviewing bios will help you formulate ideas for your Author Biography. Following is what my Author bio looks like on Amazon.com.

https://www.amazon.com/Not-Tree-Eric-Otis-Simmons/dp/1720692300/ref=sr_1_1?s=books&ie=UTF8&qid=1538669573&sr=1-1

- Read articles about Indie Authors who have had success. Their stories will keep you motivated and inspired. One piece that I found particularly interesting was an Entreprenuer.com article written by Rob Dircks entitled, "5 Things This Self-Published Author Did to Sell Over 20,000 Books With Almost No Money." The item is about Rob's first self-published book, and he highlights things he did to help drive the book's success. While Rob's achievement with his first book is more of an "outlier," I feel, it illustrates that with a good book, a solid marketing plan, and determination, one can achieve self-publishing success.

## Beware the Sharks

In Statista's article, "U.S. Book Industry - Statistics and Facts," revenue from the global book publishing market is forecast to grow from around 113 billion U.S. dollars in 2015 to about 123 billion U.S. dollars by 2020. Revenue from the industry is projected to reach nearly 44 billion in the U.S. by 2020.

In a 2018 UKSG article, "Growth and maturity in the self-publishing industry," from 2011 to 2016, print books increased from 158,972 to 638,624: an increase of 479,652 or 301% and e-books grew from 88,238 to 148,311: an increase of 60,073 or 68%. The combined print and e-book numbers rose from 247,210 to 786,935: an increase of 539,725 or 218%. Why is this important, and why am I sharing these numbers? Well, where money and growth reside, there are bound to be sharks!

Like great white sharks hunting to feast on baby seals who haven't yet acquired the skills or experience to learn how

## Chapter 3 — Beware the Sharks

to outmaneuver and outswim their predator, the same can perhaps be said about book industry preyers on new self-published authors. You will find there are a lot of "free" and seemingly, "too good to be true" options available to "self-publishers." They may come from editors to book cover designers, to companies who offer to print and distribute your book, you name it. There are a lot of gimmicks and promises out there, such as guarantees that you'll sell a certain number of books, etc. Some offers are almost comical. In Chapter 7, I'll share with you how I learned my book was being "Pirated," as a result of a "free" offer I had previously taken advantage of and what steps I undertook to resolve the "pirating" matter. Remember, when you come across a "Free" offer to help you publish your book, be sure to read the fine print.

    To avoid getting "scammed," or "bitten" if you will, I recommend you go with known entities with proven track records and those whose reputations are on the line. Once you have a clearer understanding of the self-publishing market, you can always go back to lesser-known entities that may be growing and are indeed reputable.

# Chapter 4
# Writing Your Book

Writing your first book will be one of the most challenging, yet rewarding things you most likely will have ever done. It will take planning, preparation, organization, patience, creativity, and stick-to-itiveness on your part. You will find yourself sweating the smallest of details with your book as you strive to produce a quality piece of work that readers will enjoy. Somewhere I read, "Seek not to write a good book, but rather, seek to write a great book!"

## Goal Setting

As previously shared, for my first book, I had two clearly defined Goals. They were: 1). Provide my children with information about their Family Tree and heritage, and 2). Share my "Life Story" to inspire and motivate others, particularly young Black men and woman, who like me may have been raised by a single parent. An unwritten Goal, but one always at the forefront of my mind, was to write a book that flowed. In other words, I wanted the reader to transition from one event to another as if they were there. My Goals for this book are to 1). Provide you with a "resource" or "primer" to help you get started self-publishing. 2). Provide you with a "tool" you can refer back to during the various stages of your book writing. 3). Take you through steps I went through when I wrote my first book and share some of my strategies, which I believe helped drive my first book's success and 4). Keep the manuscript to under 100 pages so you can focus your time on writing your first self-published book.

As you prepare to write your book, do write down your goals. They will give you something to strive toward and help keep you focused.

## Planning, Preparation, and Organization

Last year, when I was getting up to speed on self-publishing, I noticed a recurring theme from successful Indie Authors. They tended to talk about the planning, preparation, and organizing they go through before starting their writing project. Just like planning a vacation trip by car, they were mapping out their route to help them get to their final destination successfully. In this case, the endpoint is a well-written book.

When you begin your book writing process, if you're like me, your mind might be all over the place. To get yourself organized, I suggest writing your main thoughts down on paper as to what you plan to cover in your book. For me, creating an outline works best. For this book, I jotted down the most important things, in bullet point format, that I wanted to convey to you and put the information in a Microsoft Word document I titled, "Outline for How to Self-Publish." My bulleted items would become my Chapters, and information underneath my bullets would be the contents of a particular Chapter. Having my outline in Word allowed me to move things around until they made sense to me, from an organization standpoint. As I completed portions of this book, I would highlight the relevant section(s) from the bulleted list in my outline to denote; I had finished that particular portion of the book. This "checking off" of my completed work also served as a "reward," in that I could see my progress.

## Font Selection

Admittedly, when I began writing my first book, I didn't realize how much emphasis the book industry places on fonts or their importance. The Internet is full of information about suggested interior and exterior (i.e., front and back book cover) fonts for books. What I found during my research last year was, certain fonts for the interior of a book are more acceptable, literary-wise, for particular genres. To illustrate, in an InDesignSkills article, "Best Fonts for Books: The Only 5 Fonts You'll Ever Need," the site suggests:

1. For Literary Fiction: Baskerville
2. For Romantic Fiction: Sabon
3. For Thrillers and Airport Page-Turners: Garamond
4. For Academic Non-Fiction: Caslon
5. For General Interest: Utopia

While the above list is just one opinion, I suggest you try to determine the interior and exterior fonts used by Authors of best-selling books in your genre. It's best to stay status quo with fonts used in your genre, I feel. If you're using Microsoft Word to create your book, the font you decide on may not be available with Word. As a result, you may have to download a font or fonts, for perhaps a fee.

Following my review of fonts for the interior of my Memoir, I settled on Garamond. Admittedly, I didn't put a lot of consideration into the font I chose for the exterior of "Not Far From The Tree." Reason being, I was in a rush to get my book out and failed to understand how important the book's cover is. I ended up using Calibri as the font, and it seemed to work out okay, but I should have used a graphic designer for my cover versus doing it myself. After my book had been out for one year, I turned to a graphic designer to redo the front cover. The individual had done a lot of book covers for Authors and seemed knowledgeable about fonts for specific genres. I found the designer for a reasonable price on www.fiverr.com. The site was referred to me by fellow self-publisher Michael McCree. The fonts that the designer used for my updated cover were Trajan pro, Arial, and Great Vibe. Two of the fonts I'd never heard of but based on feedback I've received about the cover my new fonts seem to work well together.

If you are unable to determine the interior and exterior fonts used in "top selling" books, it is probably best to stay with traditional fonts like those listed or suggested on another "recommended fonts" list you might find. If you use someone to design your book cover, who has worked with other

Authors, they should be able to recommend appropriate fonts for your genre. The moral of the font story is to stay traditional for the interior and use a pro, if you can afford it, for your outer covers.

## Setting Aside Time to Write

Your book is a project. Hence, I would encourage you to try to develop a routine you can stick to when writing your work. For my first self-published piece, I established a habit of working on the book at least 4 hours a day. No matter what time of day or night, I would start my writing, I would try to write for 4 hours and take a break whenever I felt I needed one. You may not always meet your writing time goals, and that's okay because there will be times when you exceed your goals. When this happens, and I refer to this as getting into a "writing zone," your words on paper will start flowing so well, you won't want to stop writing. The whole idea is to try to build some structure and discipline around your writing so that you can ultimately complete your finished book.

# Tools to Help You Write

## Speech to Text Software

When I sat down to write my first book, it didn't take me long to realize I was going nowhere fast. The problem I was having was I never learned how to type! I am, admittedly, a "hunt and peck" typist. That's a tremendous disadvantage if you are trying to write a book! Fortunately for me, I found some speech to text software I had purchased several years back for the very purpose of getting around my typing deficiency. The application I had was Dragon NaturallySpeaking, now Dragon Professional by Nuance. I even found the headset I had purchased to use with the software. When I first started using the program, I was surprised by how easy it was for me to train the application to recognize my voice. The software also captured information on my writing style from previous emails and Word documents I had written.

The infusion of speech to text technology for my book, caused my writing speed to go from me being the tortoise to the hare, metaphorically speaking. The ability to articulate my thoughts and have the computer type the words out for me sent my productivity through the roof! I was able to complete large sections of my book at a time after I began using speech to text software. As a result, I highly recommend using this type of technology or something similar, to help speed you along your way.

## Microsoft Office Dictation

Microsoft had speech to text capability in Word when I wrote my first book, but since I had become familiar with Dragon NaturallySpeaking, I didn't see a need to change. For this book, I used Microsoft Office Dictation, which was a part of my Office 365 subscription, and while I found it pretty easy to use, it wasn't quite as intuitive as the Nuance product, I feel.

## Grammarly

I don't recall how I found out about Grammarly, but I'm sure glad I did! Grammarly is an application that automatically detects potential grammar, spelling, punctuation, word choice, and style mistakes in writing. Grammarly's algorithms flag potential issues in text and suggest context-specific corrections for grammar, spelling, wordiness, style, punctuation, and plagiarism. It is the tool I use for editing and sentence structure assistance. The product has saved me money, I feel, regarding me not having to hire a professional proofreader or editor. If you struggle with your writing, however, by all means, do use someone familiar with book editing. I still have people proofread my book when I can find such a resource for free.

I started out using Grammarly on a monthly payment basis but became so impressed with its accuracy, I purchased an annual license and now use the application for my emails, my book's Facebook and Twitter pages, etc. So, if you want to keep your costs down, think about using Grammarly or a similar package as your first line of defense for "editing." Then, if you feel you still need an editor, hopefully, you won't have to pay quite as much because Grammarly will have done a lot of the heavy lifting for you. As I was writing this book, I learned ALLi also recommends Grammarly.

## Strategies for Your Book

### Set a Target Number of Pages

When I was writing my Memoir, it became painfully obvious the book could get quite large. I would imagine anyone writing an autobiography could go on and on. At some point, I made the conscious decision to try to keep the book to 200 pages. Part of my rationale was, I didn't want my prospective reader to get bored. Another was, as the size of a book increases, so does the printing cost. Depending on the company you choose to print your book, the cost goes up at a certain number of pages. For my first book, I noticed most of the printing companies I was considering had a pretty good price increase at 250 pages.

My decision to have a "targeted number of pages" proved to be a great "discipline check" for me. Having a self-imposed page limit forced me to take out extraneous information and caused me to be more concise and to the point. I missed my objective by 20 pages with my first book, but I didn't get to what could have easily been a 300 plus page manuscript and a higher price tag to print my book.

If you find yourself in a position where you feel you can't stop at a certain number of pages, think about writing a series. They tend to do well in the book world.

## Keep Writing When You "Get on a Roll"

Some days you will get on a roll, and you will want to keep writing. By all means, continue to do so, even if the material isn't relevant to where you are in the book. When I have information that doesn't appear to fit, I put it at the end of the book on a page or pages I call a "placeholder." Interestingly, a lot of the information in my "placeholder" wound up in my first book. The material turned out to be necessary, after all. It just wasn't needed in the place I was writing in the book at the time.

## Proofread Your Work Regularly

While proofreading your work may be common sense, it can't be overstated. I reread my Memoir so many times; I got tired of reading my material. You will be surprised at things you will catch and that you can improve upon in your book by merely taking the time to proofread your work. Remember, your book is a reflection of you, and you want to be sure you are putting your best foot forward.

## Dealing with Writer's Block

To get a feel for how significant writer's block can be, Google the term. You'll get about 18.7 million hits! Writer's block affects every Author. It hit me hard when I got to the "Fonts" section of this book. I had to get away from writing for four days! In my view, when one is writing a book, their concentration level is so high, and they are so focused, they begin to tire and wear down a bit. When this happens, I believe it creates writer's block. With my Memoir, I experienced writer's block so severely that I had to get away from writing for two weeks. Had a friend not called to ask me how I was doing with the book, I might have taken another week or two off. Some of the things I believe you and I can do to address writer's block is to take frequent breaks. Perhaps going for a walk, watching some TV, or rewarding ourselves when we complete a certain number of pages or reach a milestone we've set will help. The key, perhaps, is to engage in another type of activity so we can "break the monotony" and get out of our funk. Remembering our "purpose for writing" will also help get us back on track. So, when you hit the wall, and experience writer's block, know you're not alone, and it won't last forever. Once your battery is recharged, you'll be back on your way to writing.

## Use of Third Party Material

If you use material from someone else, such as photos, articles, etc., be sure to denote the originator someplace in your book, such as the "References" section. Just because the material is in the "Public Domain," such as the Internet, doesn't necessarily mean it isn't copyright protected. When I identify photos or images on the Worldwide Web that I would like to use, before I do so, I choose "Settings" under the Google search bar and select "Advanced search" which when clicked, takes me to a screen named "Advanced Image Search." Near the bottom of the screen, there is a "usage rights" line item that has a drop-down menu. From the menu choices, I then select "free to use, share or modify, even commercially." This way, I will receive "hits" on items where the originator has granted use. There have also been times when I have reached out directly to the originator of a photo or image via phone or email to request permission to use their work. If I don't get a return call or email back, I note it in a folder on my computer. Should something come up later, and I am requested to remove the item, I will at least be able to share, I attempted to contact the owner. It is better to reach out to the material's owner, if you feel it's warranted or when you're unsure about usage, rather than risk copyright infringement.

# Chapter 5
# Setting up Your Book Business

At some point, preferably before you've finished your book, you will need to begin setting up your "book business." It doesn't have to be anything elaborate, but you will need some type of "business" structure in place, if for no other reason than for tax purposes. It's important to remember when your book is sold, each sale is reported as revenue to the IRS by the selling party. Also, each of the Companies you select to have print and distribute your book will ask you for things such as your Taxpayer ID or perhaps your social security number, the bank account number that you want your royalties to go to and the like. For me, it was easier to set up a small business, so transactions related to my book wouldn't get intertwined with my personal checking accounts. Imagine trying to separate your book revenue and expenses from your personal checking account transactions during tax season!

I chose to Incorporate to reduce my personal liability, but you can set up a Sole Proprietorship, Partnership, Limited Liability Company (LLC), etc., depending on what works best for you. If you are unsure, seek advice from someone familiar with the various business types and their advantages and disadvantages.

For my accounting, I chose a free online service for small businesses called Wave, which also offers invoicing and receipt scanning. The software is tied to my business checking account and allows me to keep up with my revenues, expenses, profit, and loss, etc. I found the software to be quite beneficial during tax season. There are other products out there like QuickBooks and TurboTax that you can use for your accounting as well.

From an accounting standpoint, one of the expenses that can be easily overlooked is your business mileage, which can add up quickly, especially if you travel to events like book shows. To give you a perspective, for my book and Website design business, I drove a total of 4,346 business miles in 2017. The way the IRS currently calculates business mileage, my deduction was slightly over $2,000 in mileage expense for the year! I use an App called Hurdlr, which can track my mileage from the time I leave home to my return when I'm doing book-related business. There are numerous Apps out there to help you track your mileage, so don't forget to get one.

# Chapter 6

## Identifying Initial Service Providers

### Print Books - Paperback/Hard Copy

After you have finished writing your book, reviewed and edited it, decided on a cover and felt you have your final product ready, you will be at a point where you will need to make some decisions about who you want to have print and distribute your book if you haven't done so already. Companies that offer book printing and distribution services may refer to themselves as Self-Publishing Platform and Print on Demand (POD) providers or similar. I'll use the terms "provider" and "service provider" going forward to denote companies that offer Self-Publishing Platform and Print on Demand (POD) services. It's important to note, some of these companies will also allow you to also sell your book on their websites (ex. Amazon) as well.

The provider selection process may seem daunting at first, but there are resources available to help you narrow down your initial selections. An aid I ended up using to decide on my providers was a document developed by ALLi called, "Best

Chapter 6  Identifying Initial Service Providers

and Worst Self-Publishing Services Reviewed & Rated by the Alliance of Independent Authors." The resource uses color codes to rate companies and is based on ALLi's appraisals of multiple criteria, including pricing and value, quality of service, contract terms and rights, transparency, accountability, and customer satisfaction. Green denotes companies whose services have been vetted by ALLi and meet the organization's Code of Standards. Blue indicates companies which have been observed to behave ethically and professionally, with pricing and value in line with industry norms, and red highlights companies whose services do not align with ALLi's Code of Standards. I view the companies in red as "do not go near" because these may be some of the "sharks" I alluded to earlier. You'll notice there are a lot of companies "in the red" on the document's list! Following is a screenshot of a portion of the tool:

Chapter 6                    Identifying Initial Service Providers

| | | |
|---|---|---|
| Partnership between Alliant University and **Author Solutions** | | |
| Amazon (CreateSpace) | 🔗 ★ Partner Member | |
| Read our comparison of **Ingram Spark vs. CreateSpace**, and learn how you can **use both services** to leverage the strengths of each. | | |
| Amazon (KDP) | 🔗 ★ Partner Member | |
| Read our comparison of publishing platforms in **Amazon vs. Apple** | | |
| America Star Books | ⚠ Watchdog Advisory | Legal, Value, Communication, Service, Transparency, Marketing, Quality |
| Formerly PublishAmerica, a vanity press with a staggering number of **complaints**. | | |
| Amnet Systems | 🔗 ★ Partner Member | |
| Amolibros | 🔗 ★ Partner Member | |
| Anthemion Software | 🔗 ★ Partner Member | |
| Apple (iBooks) | 🔗 ✓ Recommended | |
| Read our comparison of publishing platforms in **Amazon vs. Apple** | | |
| Archway Publishing | ⚠ Watchdog Advisory | Legal, Value, Communication, Service, Transparency, Marketing, Quality |

When I was reviewing providers, I ran across well-known companies such as Amazon and Barnes & Noble, but others kept coming up, that I had never heard of. A few were CreateSpace, Nook Press, and Ingram. I remember thinking, "Who are these people, and why have I never heard of them?" In the self-publishing industry, they are known entities. CreateSpace was a for "free" service provider that Amazon acquired in 2005. In August 2018, Amazon merged its CreateSpace and Kindle Direct Publishing (KDP) business units into one service, KDP, which is also free. NOOK Press, now Barnes & Noble Press, is Barnes & Noble's free self-publishing offering and Ingram Content Group, or Ingram, offers a self-publishing service through its IngramSpark business for a fee of, currently, $49 annually. I found Ingram through my research on providers who had a strong presence with libraries, which was a market I had planned on targeting. There are a number of other self-publishing service providers in the ALLi document from which to choose. I chose the above three due to their brand recognition in the self-publishing industry, and/or market strength in areas I planned to try to sell my book. Each of the companies has potential access to millions of online customers and thousands of retailers, libraries, and bookstores.

Starting out and even now, I find the various relationships between the companies involved in printing and distributing books to be confusing. At a "high level," the following "flow" chart is my attempt at showing how self-published books ultimately get to customers.

Chapter 6                Identifying Initial Service Providers

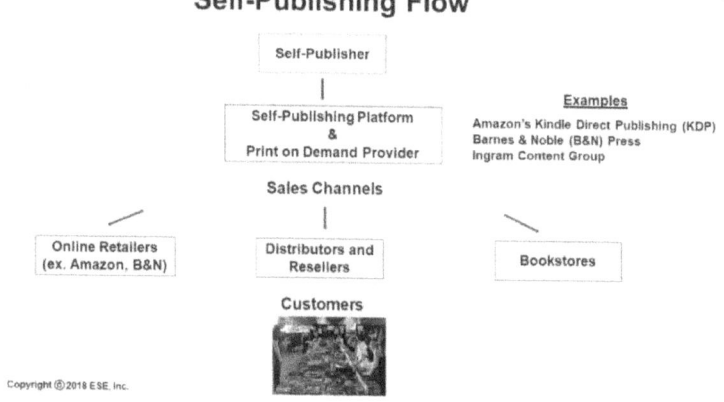

## eBook

The service provider(s) you choose for your paperback and/or hard copy book will more than likely offer eBook printing and distribution as well. I initially used KDP for my eBook printing and distribution due to Amazon's brand recognition and later added other companies. Two other companies that I found in the ALLi document with good reviews were Smashwords and Draft2Digital. Both of whom I hadn't heard of previously.

Smashwords has been in the industry since 2008 and offers free eBook publishing and distribution services. They proclaim to be, "the world's largest distributor of Indie eBooks." They have partnerships with Apple, Kobo, and Barnes & Noble, to name a few. Smashwords' website states they are used by over 130,000 Authors.

ALLi's review of Draft2Digital (D2D) is also favorable, and they are another free eBook service provider. After working with them for a while now, I view them as an up and coming business in what I call the "next wave" of eBook self-publishing service providers. In an August 2017 Good eReader article entitled, "Draft2Digital is the Best Ebook Distribution Platform for Indie Authors," Michael Kozlowski describes D2D as one of the rising superstars Indie Authors should know about. D2D has virtually the same partnerships (i.e., Apple, Kobo, Barnes & Noble, etc.) as Smashwords.

I didn't start selling my eBook directly through Barnes and Noble until this year because both Smashwords and D2D had partnerships with them. Arrangements such as these get into the "confusing" relationships I mentioned earlier. By the time I was ready to incorporate Ingram for my eBook, I had learned they charge $25 when you don't combine your print book and eBook with them at the outset.

The reason why I didn't initially incorporate other companies along with KDP for my first eBook was due to an

"Exclusivity" clause in their "Expanded Distribution" offering which prohibits you from selling your eBook through another provider. I will go into more detail about this in the next section.

## Review Your Provider Agreements

When you decide on a provider, do take the time to read through their agreements. You may find there's a "catch," if you will, that may prohibit or limit you in some way.

### Exclusivity Arrangements

Some of the agreements you will come across may contain exclusivity clauses. Amazon's KDP Select program, for example, is an exclusive offering which opens up your eBook to the Kindle world and provides royalties of up to 70%. Per KDP's website, "When you choose to enroll your book in KDP Select, you're committing to making the digital format of that book available exclusively through KDP. During the period of exclusivity, you cannot distribute your book digitally anywhere else, including on your website, blogs, etc." Ouch! If you want to sell your eBook to the Apple

Chapter 6                        Identifying Initial Service Providers

marketplace or through Ingram, you can't while you are in the KDP Select program! Currently, KDP Select requires you to stay enrolled in the program for three (3) months at a time. Afterward, you can opt out or continue to remain in the program for 3-month intervals. For my first book, I stayed in the program for six (6) months. The draw was Amazon's reach! My "enrollment" in the KDP program is what kept me from offering my eBook through other providers initially.

Over time, I grew agitated about not being able to sell my eBook to other companies offering non-Kindle eBook devices such as Apple. Here's why. According to a 2017 report by Authorearnings.com, eBook sales were as follows:

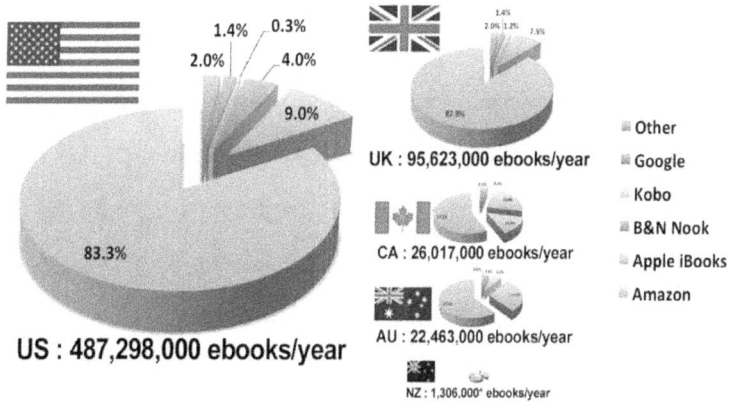

Chapter 6  Identifying Initial Service Providers

While the chart clearly shows Amazon's dominance in the eBook marketplace, I picked up on the 13.3% sales per year by Apple Books, Barnes & Noble, and Kobo. The percentage was too large for me to ignore. "Why should I leave potential revenue on the table?" was my thinking then and now.

"Should I Stay In Kindle KDP Select Or Open Publish?" is an article written by Just Publishing Advice owner Derek Haines. In it, Haines provides his perspective and shares he moves in and out of KDP, so he can use other providers that support non-Kindle devices. I do the same thing as Haines. My desire to sell my eBook through other channels was the primary cause for me dropping out of KDP Select after six months. Personally, I don't like exclusive agreements because they restrict you to a specific provider. By understanding the provider's terms and conditions, however, you'll be able to decide when you can opt in or out.

When I learned Ingram also distributed to the Apple Books market, I jumped at the opportunity to "sign up." Upon reviewing their eBook agreement, however, I came across an exclusivity "clause," which prohibits selling your eBook through other channels such as Amazon. The clause was Ingram's version of KDP Select, in my view. These type of "catch 22" scenarios, if you will, can leave an Indie Author feeling like their hands are being tied. Situations like these are where your "creativity" (i.e., opting in and out) will need to come into play.

## Impact of Free ISBNs

The larger service providers will typically offer you free ISBNs for your print book and eBook. While "Free" is a good thing, you can easily wind up having multiple ISBNs for the same title! For my eBooks, I don't mind this quandary as much, but for my print book(s), I prefer a "Universal ISBN" so that my customers can refer to one identification number, versus multiple ones, to find my material. Multiple ISBNs may end up being unavoidable, however, due to "exclusivity" clauses in provider agreements. In my case, my Memoir has several ISBNs. Some are free, and one is a Universal ISBN that I purchased with the hope of using it across all of my providers one day. Just remember, if you use a Universal ISBN, you'll likely be prohibited from participating in "exclusive" offerings that might reach a broader audience.

# Chapter 7
# Pricing Your Book

After I finished writing my first book, I agonized over what the price should be. If I priced the manuscript too high, I wondered if people would people buy it. If my price was too low, I felt I could find myself missing out on additional revenue. As it turns out, service providers allow you to change your price at your discretion. Typically, once you make a price change, the update occurs within 24 to 72 hours. With Ingram, price changes are now active weekly versus monthly, which was formerly the case.

The way I came up with the price for my first book was by following a suggestion in an article I read which recommended going onto Amazon.com and reviewing the costs of books in your genre. When I did, I noted the pricing of books that were doing exceptionally well and ones not doing so well. Then, I honed in on the pricing associated with about ten books that had a lot of reviews and were rated 4 or more stars. I scrolled down to the bottom of the page of each book looking for the ones that had roughly the same number of pages as my book so that I could make an "apples to apples" comparison. I took the average price of the books that had a similar number of pages as mine to come up with my initial price for, "Not Far From the Tree," which I ended up releasing at $12.99.

Because of your ability to quickly and easily change your price with your providers, there's no need, I feel, to be overly concerned about your initial pricing. If sales aren't going as well as you would like, think about doing a price change with just one provider to see what the impact is before you incorporate a price change with the others. Typically, when I make a price change, I do it across the board with all of my providers just for consistency purposes.

## Shipping and Handling

One of the things I did not take into account when I came up with a price for my Memoir was providers' shipping and handling charges. If it costs anywhere from $3 to $7, for example, for shipping and handling charges, the average is $5. Now, my $12.99 book is costing a customer $17.99! When I realized this, it gave me heartburn. While I felt then and now, my book is worth the price I am offering, the additional charges may make the book seem "pricey" to some. So,

Chapter 7                                            Pricing Your Book

remember to consider shipping and handling when you develop your book's price.

# Chapter 8

## Formatting Your Book for Printing

After you have written and edited your book, identified your providers, and decided on a price for your book, you will need to prepare your document for uploading to your service providers so they can print it and get it ready for distribution.

### Print Book

Most of the partners you'll come across will accept your book in PDF format. Some, like Barnes & Noble, will also import Microsoft Word documents. Uploading the "file" in PDF format should go smoothly for you. If a problem occurs, the providers' platform tool will let you know. You may have to go through several iterations if you have formatting or other issues associated with your submission before your document is accepted. When it is, you will be provided a draft for review. Once you're satisfied, your book is ready; you will authorize your provider to begin printing and distributing your book!

Although each service provider's platforms are different, the steps for getting your book ready for printing and distribution are, for the most part, the same. The "steps" typically involve:

1. **Setup.** In this step, you will upload your book and its cover.
2. **Review.** You will have an opportunity to review the output and make modifications.
3. **Distribute.** Here you will have an opportunity to choose the channels that you would like to have distribute and/or sell your book. You'll also provide your book's price and information about the book (i.e., the book's metadata) which I'll cover in the next topic.
4. **Convert to eBook** which I'll cover later in this Chapter.

## Metadata

Before uploading your book to your provider, I suggest you have your Metadata and search words ready. Per IngramSpark in, "The Basics of Book Metadata and

Keywords," your book's metadata will consist of basic things such as your title, author name, author bio, book description, publication date, etc. Keywords are one or more words used to indicate the content of your book." Each of your partners' platforms will ask you for this type of information during your interaction with their platform.

To help me with my author bio and book description, I went online and reviewed the biographies and book descriptions of some best-selling authors to get a feel for the type of information they were presenting to their audience. For my book's description, which I put on the back cover of my Memoir, I wanted to give the prospective buyer a quick "snapshot" of the book's contents. Your book description should be attention-getting and cause the potential buyer to want to purchase your book.

For my publication date, I used the date of my final submission to the first service provider that I chose to print and distribute my book.

## Keywords

Desirous of wanting everyone in the world to be able to find my first book in a Google search, I spent an inordinate amount of time, trying to come up with the "perfect" keywords. At the time, I didn't realize how easy it would be for me to go back to my providers' platforms and change my keywords if I felt they weren't working. To come up with my keywords, I did an "exercise" you may find helpful. I used Google Trends to find out how popular the keywords were that I had chosen for my book. The site shows trends of a word or words going back to 2004 and can drill down to word(s) popularity by state level. I got so carried away with the tool that I developed a spreadsheet and began to rank my keywords, to find the "perfect" keywords for my book. To illustrate how Google Trends works, I entered the search words, "how to books," and got the following "trend line" result:

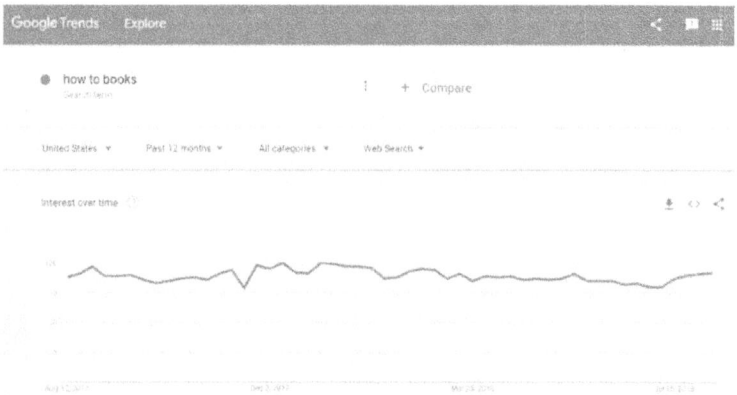

The popularity of the phrase, "how to books" in Google searches appear to have an average score of around 85 out of 100, over the past year. I view 85 as a good score, so I'll probably use the words "how to books" in my keyword choices. Such popularity leaves me optimistic my new "how to book" on self-publishing stands a good chance of being found in Google searches. Another one of my keywords for this book will be, "self-publishing" (probably with and without the dash). I believe you get the gist.

The importance of keywords cannot be overstated because they will be how your customers will find your book. When thinking about keywords, try to put yourself in the potential customer's shoes. What search words are they likely to use to find a book such as yours? The search words you come up with should be close to what you think the potential buyer of your book would choose. If over time, you feel you aren't getting enough hits on Google with your keywords, you can go back and change them.

## Front, Back, and Spine

Uploading your front cover, spine, and back cover, which I will refer to collectively as "cover," to your provider,

Chapter 8                         Formatting Your Book for Printing

may be more of a challenge if you try to do it manually, versus using the providers' tools. For this book, I played around with KDP's "Cover Creator" and found the tool to be easy to use. If you decide to take on uploading the cover yourself, you'll need to make sure it fits properly on the provider's template, should they have one, for the size of your book. Following is the template and subsequent cover for my first book which I uploaded manually:

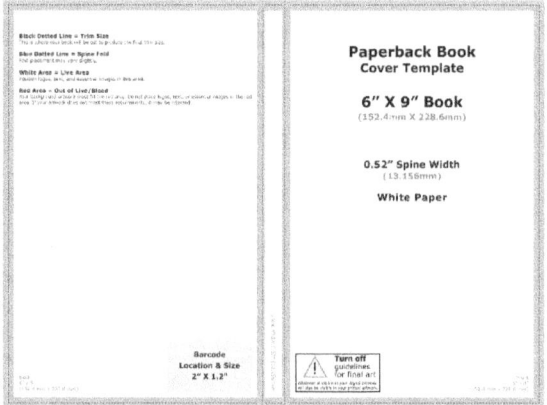

Chapter 8                Formatting Your Book for Printing

For this book, I used my providers' tools versus the manual approach.

## eBook – MOBI and ePub Formats

There are various types of eBook formats. Some of the most popular ones are ePub, MOBI, AZW, and PDF. I'll address the two I believe you'll run across the most with your providers. They are MOBI and ePub. I view these two eBook formats as analogous to what we referred to in the computer industry as "open" and "closed" architectures. To me, MOBI is a "closed" architecture because it can only be used by a particular device or type of device. ePub is more of an "open" architecture because it can be used by different devices. MOBI is the format used by Amazon for its Kindle e-Readers, and ePub, which is regarded by some experts as the most popular of the two, is used by Apple for its devices, Barnes & Noble for its Nook e-Readers, and others.

KDP's platform takes care of converting your print book to the MOBI format for you. To get your book into ePub format, you will have to use your partners' tool or do it yourself. I manually converted my first book to ePub and found the exercise to be painful.

As I was writing this book, I decided to submit, "Not Far From The Tree" to Barnes & Noble for ePub conversion so that I could put the subsequent eBook on sale with B&N. I uploaded the Word document of my book to B&N's conversion tool, and I must say, I was pleased with the tool's "ease of use." I didn't like where the tool placed my Dedication page; however, so I went back to my Word document and added an extra line before the Dedication page and resubmitted the "file." This time, the page was placed where I wanted. I submitted the book for final processing, and despite B&N's disclaimer that it could take up to seventy-two hours to process, the book was ready and on sale when I woke up the next morning.

Chapter 8　　　　　　　　　Formatting Your Book for Printing

If you are a do it yourself-er, you can use free software such as Calibre to convert your Word document to ePub. Calibre is a cross-platform open-source suite of e-Book software. I ran a test and uploaded my first book to Calibre to give you my thoughts about the software. When I converted my Memoir to ePub, I ran into a problem with one picture which the tool had turned sideways. It took me a few attempts before I realized the software had an option for resizing photos. Once I resized the image, I was pleased with the ePub output.

To summarize, there are tools available to you, provider and non-provider wise, that are available to help you successfully convert your book to ePub format.

## Beware of Online ePub Conversion Tools

I would encourage you to use the ePub conversion tools of your service provider or a free software application like Calibre versus converting your book to ePub online. Here's why. About six (6) months after my first book had been published, I did a Google search on the title to see how many times my book would appear. Lo and behold, I saw an Ad for my Memoir being sold in PDF format. I was dumbfounded because I had not made, "Not Far From The Tree" available for sale to anyone in PDF format! I followed the link associated with the Ad, and sure enough, someone was trying to sell my copyrighted book without my permission. I was shocked to find my book had been "Pirated!" How could this happen, you ask?

When I initially tried converting my first book to ePub, I experimented with a "free" online conversion tool. Other than the providers I had chosen to work with, the online tool was the only other source that had a copy of my book. I'm convinced this is how the "Pirated" copy got out. Furious, I called a lawyer and explained my situation. The lawyer was all too familiar with the scenario and suggested I issue what's called a DMCA Takedown Notice to the offending individual(s) associated with the site offering my book for sale. DMCA is the acronym for **Digital Millennium Copyright Act.** Under the act, any owner of content has the right to process a takedown notice against a website owner and/or an Online Service Provider (ex. ISP, hosting company, etc.) if the content owner's property is found online without their permission. I was so upset about the matter; I ended up sending ten emails to the offender! How dare someone take advantage of the blood, sweat, and tears I had poured into my book and then try to turn around and sell it for profit and without my knowledge. The story gets better. This same individual(s), as best as I can determine, has different websites where they run the same scheme. After chasing them for several months, I discovered Google has a site where you can file a DMCA through them, which is what I do now. Imagine the offender's surprise when they got a notice from Google who can remove the offender's URL from Google searches. Should, heaven forbid, someone "Pirates" your book, the Google DMCA Takedown Notice website address is: https://www.google.com/webmasters/tools/dmca-notice?pli=1. A snapshot of the "DMCA" page follows.

> **Google**
>
> Copyright Removal
>
> Report alleged copyright infringement: Web Search
>
> It is our policy to respond to notices of alleged infringement that comply with the Digital Millennium Copyright Act applicable intellectual property laws. Our response may include removing or disabling access to material claimed response to such a notice, we may notify the owner or administrator of the affected site or content so that he or s which we act, including by sending a copy of the notice to one or more third parties or making it available to the p
>
> **Infringement Notification**
>
> To file a notice of infringement with us, you may use the form provided below
>
> IMPORTANT: Misrepresentations made in your notice regarding whether material or activity is infringing may exp consider copyright defenses, limitations or exceptions before sending a notice. In one case involving online cont the U.S. fair use doctrine. Accordingly, if you are not sure whether material available online infringes your copyrig
>
> * Required field
>
> **Contact Information**
>
> First name: *
>
> Last name: *
>
> Company Name:

Some self-published Authors don't mind if their books get "pirated" because they feel there is value in having as many copies of their book out in the marketplace as possible. Well, I beg to differ!!

# Chapter 9

## Marketing Your Book

The fact that your service providers are placing your book in various markets for prospective customers to have access to does not imply that they or the entities that they make your book available to, such as retailers, are promoting your book. Marketing and promotion of the product you have created as a self-publisher is up to you. So, where do you begin?

As an immensely excited new Indie Author, I started by marketing and promoting my new book to family and friends. In my enthusiasm, following my book's release, and in the first year, I gave away 35 books, and 2 of those were to a husband and his wife! When I added it up, my generosity cost me $245. Think about this. I currently charge $12 for my Memoir when I sell it at a book show. If I had not given away 35 copies of my book and sold it directly, I could have made $420! By not setting a limit on my book "giveaways," I learned a hard lesson, and that's why I'm sharing it with you. Don't get so carried away about your new book that you overlook what "giveaways" may be costing you financially. I suggest you set aside a low number of books, say 10-20 for example, for family and friends. With such a small quantity for "giveaways," you might upset a family member or friend along the way, but you won't be losing your shirt appeasing people.

## Determine Your Target Market

Imagine your book's genre as the "landscape" in which it resides. Then picture the sales opportunity for your work as an iceberg of which the tip is 10% of the overall size. Your "true opportunity" therein, lies in the 90% that's "hidden" underneath the surface! Using this analogy, family and friends represent the tip of your sales opportunity. While they are the most readily visible and available, they represent the area in which you will have little or no sales. The "hidden" opportunity rests in the markets you "target" to sell and promote your book to and is where you should spend the bulk of your time.

The following graphic shows some of the "target" markets I chose for my first book.

Chapter 9 — Creating Awareness

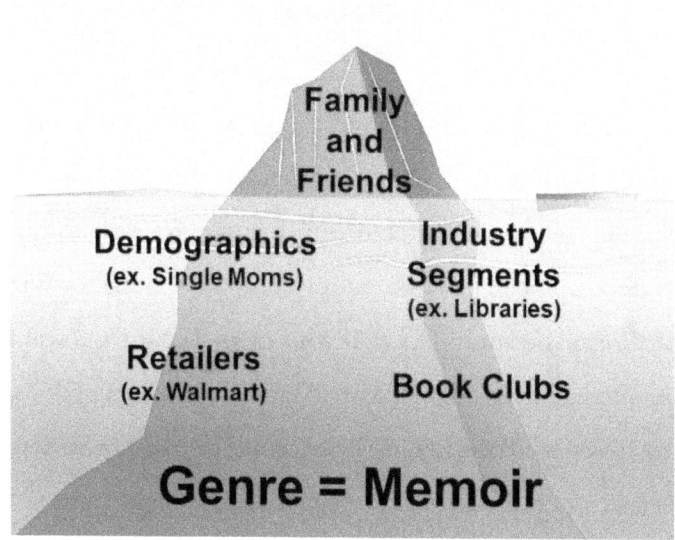

## Creating Awareness

Now that you've determined who your "target audience" will be, you will need to come up with a plan on how you will make them aware of your book. I recommend at a minimum; you have a website and Facebook business page for your book. If you're familiar with Twitter, I suggest a page for your book there as well.

## Website

There are many ways to get your website up and running for your book. You can hire someone to build you a site, or if you're comfortable with technology, you can use a web development platform from companies such as Wix or WordPress. Be sure to look at your overall cost for a website. Your site will need to be "hosted" and also maintained. Also, there likely will be charges from your website provider for updates to news articles and blogs that you might want to add to your site. To get an idea of the content I have on my Author's website, you can visit www.esetomes.com.

While building Author sites is not my website Company's primary focus, as a Certified Wix Webmaster, I have been contemplating building websites for self-published Authors. Should I get enough interest, I may pursue doing so. If you're interested, feel free to contact me through my www.esetomes.com website.

## Engaging Your Target Markets

Before engaging your target markets, give some thought to the who, what, when, where, why, and how. I'll use a few of the lessons I've learned from engaging Libraries, one of my target markets, to illustrate. At the onset, I did not know **Who** Libraries purchased their books from and **How** they made their buying decisions. Upon doing some research, I came across an American Library Association article entitled, "Marketing to Libraries." It mentioned, "Libraries purchase books through such companies as Baker & Taylor, Ingram Library Services, Emery-Pratt Company, and other book suppliers and wholesalers." These companies were the **Who** I was looking for regarding the sources from which Libraries purchase their books. This information also helped me to decide on using Ingram as one of my service providers to libraries. I also learned **Who** makes the purchasing decisions at a library. Depending upon the size of a facility, it could be the Head Librarian or the Collections/Acquisition Manager. Once I began engaging Librarians, some would refer me to their "Collection Development Policy," which is the guideline as to **How** a Library makes its purchasing decisions. My research also provided me with information as to **When** libraries procure. Although many buy throughout the year, I have found contacting Librarians several months before their Fiscal Year End and Fiscal Year Begin, which for many is in the June/July timeframe, is a good time to get a book in front of them.

Learning as much as you can about your target audience will help you develop effective marketing strategies.

## Advertising

In my budget for this book, I've allocated $40 for Advertising to promote it following my "formal" announcement of its's availability. I'm anticipating spending $20 each on a Facebook and Twitter Ad. While this is a low amount, my experience has been each Ad will be presented to roughly 16,000 people. My goals for the Ads will be to 1.) Create awareness about #HTSP and 2.) Drive people to the www.esetomes.com website where they will be able to learn more about the book and purchase it from the site. Note: I will have links to the book's purchasing pages on Amazon, B&N, etc. The site visitor will also be able to learn more about, "Not Far From The Tree," which could result in an additional sale from a single visit!

Admittedly, I haven't been able to identify a large number of sales attributable to my social media advertising, but the number of people the Ads will be exposed to is too large for me to ignore. Should you decide to advertise on a social media site, I suggest you start by budgeting low and then increase your budget as you begin to have sales success on these platforms. You should also target your Facebook and Twitter friends with your initial announcement about your new book. A technique that has worked for me, to keep from inundating my friends about my book, is to periodically share an update from my book's Facebook business page. "Sharing" from another site is another way to draw people to a specific location where you are promoting your book.

Depending on your budget for advertising, you can pay for Ads through your provider partners, or through magazines, or other sources you feel can help you get the word out about your book. Ultimately, you want to get to a point where the revenue from your book's sales can be used to pay for your Ads versus repeatedly having to pay out of pocket.

Remember, with your book, you've created a business and become an entrepreneur, even if you plan to write only one book. With business ownership in mind, one of your goals for your writing should be to try to turn a profit. Your advertising budget is one element of your business' expenses you want to be sure to manage appropriately.

# Chapter 10
## Managing Your Book Business

Ultimately, how you choose to run and manage your book business will depend on your time, your "management" style and other factors. I tend to keep a close eye on my "book business." Following are just a few of the things I've put in place that have helped me manage my "business."

## Book Database

I maintain an Excel spreadsheet, which is more like a "book database." In the "database," I have a tab for a sheet that has all of my providers' charges and their royalties. With this information, when I record a sale from the providers' sales report, I have set up my spreadsheet so that my royalties are automatically calculated for me. My calculation serves as a "cross-check" to the providers' report. I also have a sheet where I can see my royalties by provider, and I take that information and load it into a pie chart so that I can see where my revenue is coming from by provider in percentages. I also have a tab for a sheet that shows me my book revenues,

Chapter 10 — Managing Your Book Business

giveaways, and book ordering expenses. This way, I can see my profit/loss and compare the information with what's showing up in the Wave accounting system. Another tab is used for my various paperback and eBook ISBNs. I also keep my "To Do List" for the book in the "database." Having pertinent information about my book in one place has boosted my productivity, and I would encourage you to think about a similar setup. I'm contemplating offering the database for sale so if you're interested in this type of tool, feel free to reach out to me via www.esetomes.com.

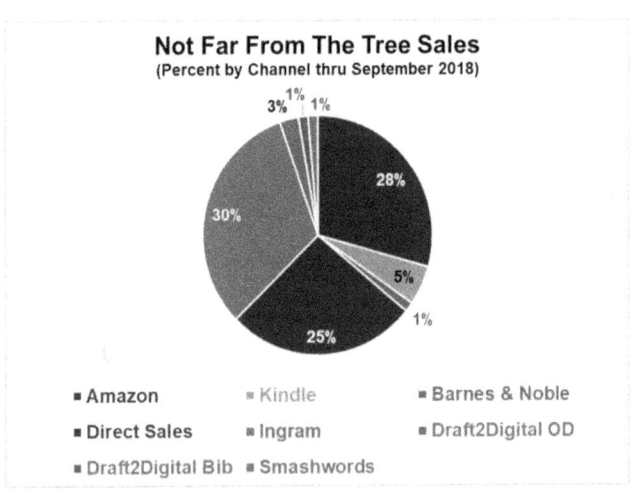

## RSS Feed

RSS stands for Rich Site Summary and is often called Really Simple Syndication. It is a type of web feed which allows users to access updates to online content in a standardized, computer-readable format. I recently started using RSS feed capability because I got tired of copying and pasting information into my various social media sites. Now, when I do a blog write-up on my book website, my Facebook, Twitter, and Amazon Author page automatically update with the same information. Talk about a time saver! Following is an example of the RSS Feed to my Amazon Author's page.

If I don't like the way a feed looks on one of my social media sites, I delete it and do my copy paste routine.

## Browser Bookmarks

For sites that you will frequently be visiting, such as your providers' sales reports, bookmark those pages so they will be readily accessible to you.

## Chapter 11

## Can You Make Money Self-Publishing?

Can you make money self-publishing? The answer is yes! I have and am continuing to do so. While the key, of course, is book sales, another critical component is managing your expenses. If you can generate sales, and keep your expenses low, your chances of earning a profit should go up. So how are Indie Authors achieving success? It varies. Some have mastered using email lists to build their client base, some have figured out specific market segments such as Libraries, and others have broken the code on their genre. Some are proficient with podcasts or blogs, while others have figured out how to get into retailers such as Walmart. The key, I feel, is to try and carve out a niche and then grow the niche. Perseverance and persistence are necessities if you want your book to be successful.

Hopefully, this "primer" will assist you in your new and exciting self-publishing journey and help you get up to speed so you can start writing your masterpiece.

Here's wishing you much success, and thank you for purchasing, "#HTSP – How to Self-Publish."

Respectfully,

# References

- Google
  - Google Trends
  - DMCA information

- Statista – "U.S. Book Industry - Statistics and Facts"
https://www.statista.com/topics/1177/book-market/

- UKSG - "Growth and maturity in the self-publishing industry"
https://www.uksg.org/sites/uksg.org/files/Editorial 412.pdf

- Merriam-Webster – definition of genre

- Wikipedia - List of writing genres
https://en.wikipedia.org/wiki/List_of_writing_genres
  - ISBN definition

- Query*Tracker* – "Top 10 Genres"
https://querytracker.net/top-10-genres.php

- The Richest.com - **Which 5 Book Genres Make The Most Money?"** by Thomas Stewart (January 31, 2014)

# References

- Nathan Bransford, "Book publishing glossary" https://blog.nathanbransford.com/book-publishing-glossary

- Bookjobs.com "Commonly Used Terms" - http://www.bookjobs.com/commonly-used-terms

- Joanna Penn – The Creative Penn website
  - https://www.thecreativepenn.com/
  - "Pros And Cons Of Traditional Publishing vs Self-Publishing"

- Alliance of Independent Authors (ALLi) https://selfpublishingadvice.org/
  - "Best and Worst Self-Publishing Services Reviewed & Rated by the Alliance of Independent Authors."

- Entrepreneur.com – "5 Things This Self-Published Author Did to Sell Over 20,000 Books With Almost No Money" https://www.entrepreneur.com/article/279385

- InDesignSkills - "Best Fonts for Books: The Only 5 Fonts You'll Ever Need" http://www.indesignskills.com/inspiration/fonts-for-books/#

- Michael McCree – Author of: "GameChanger: The Baseball Parent's Ultimate Guide" and " Mind of a Superior Hitter: The Art, Science and Philosophy"

- Authorearnings.com – "Total Ebook Unit Sales by Country and Retail Channel"

# References

http://authorearnings.com/report/february-2017/

- American Library Association – "Marketing to Libraries" http://www.ala.org/tools/libfactsheets/alalibraryfactsheet05

- Just Publishing Advice - "Should I Stay In Kindle KDP Select Or Open Publish?" by Derek Haines https://justpublishingadvice.com/should-i-stay-in-kindle-kdp-select-or-open-publish/

- Book market photo by Charlie Read on Unsplash

- Libraries purchase books through such providers as Baker & Taylor, Ingram Library Services, Emery-Pratt Company, and other book suppliers and wholesalers.

- The Basics of Book Metadata and Keywords - IngramSpark https://www.ingramspark.com/blog/the-basics-of-book-metadata-and-keywords

- 3D Issue – "What are the Differences Between .epub and .mobi?" https://www.3dissue.com/what-are-the-differences-between-epub-and-mobi/

- DMCA.com – DMCA takedown notice definition

www.ingramcontent.com/pod-product-compliance
Lightning Source LLC
Chambersburg PA
CBHW070304010526
44108CB00039B/1894